ECCLESIA MANIFESTO

DON LYNCH

Ecclesia Manifesto

Copyright 2018 by Don Lynch

All rights reserved. No part of this publication may be reproduced, stored in a retrieval system or transmitted in any form or by any means, electronic, mechanical, photocopying, recording or otherwise without the prior permission of the publisher or in accordance with the provisions of the Copyright, Designs and Patents Act 1988 or under the terms of any license permitting limited copying issued by the Copyright Licensing Agency.

Published by: MinistryMatrix Publishing

ISBN-13: 978-1724661463

ISBN-10: 1724661469

A MANIFESTO

What the Bible Says

I believe we need accelerated forward movement. I think we need a new understanding of legitimacy and authenticity. I see a restoration of kingdom principles, processes, and protocols. This is a restoration of kingdom culture. The restoration of kingdom Ecclesia begins with kingdom and the restoration of kingdom culture. I have turned to the Scriptures for this discussion. I have not added a great deal of scholarly input. I am joining a discussion.

I am more concerned with what the Bible says

than what I can make the Bible mean. I am not concerned with fitting the Bible into a schematic of manmade creation or a time-line explanation of Daniel and Jesus that some drunk lawyer came up with for a notated Bible. Nor am I interested in the continuously modified versions of end time charts that never answer to what the Bible says as much as how make all the parts fit one puzzle. The errors are vast. The exaggerations exotic. The books sold to the victimized kingdom citizens many. When a book is wrong, the author writes another and sells it to the same gullible people.

I'm ignoring it all. It is beside the point of Ecclesia anyway. Carving up *ekklesia* to fit a dispensational fantasy land of unsupportable mishmash is messy. It is mostly a waste of time. So, the elegant discourses on Hitler's mustache and the pope funny hat means nothing to defining how a kingdom ecclesia functions.

I am not the least bit concerned with making moderns happy by devising another "whatever you want, we'll get that for you" approach to church. On the other, I am not the least bit impressed with tradition and superstition. I am completely about original design and definition.

You will find no fine tuning for modern narcissism here. There is nothing new about this generation's odd ideas that a good dose of sacrifice, surrender, and submission would not fix. (By "generation" I mean every person alive right now.)

I am purposefully ignoring the modern fascination with changing everything to fit the whims of youth. Fine tuning "church-anity" to find something more appealing to moderns only makes matters worse. I have the greatest respect for the accepted distinctions and characteristics of what is commonly known as "Millennial." With due respect to the place of this age group within this generation, the joining of fathers and inheritors is God's way forward, not the alteration of everything to satisfy a need for relevancy. We do not have several generations. We have one generation composed of all who are alive at any given moment. We must bond that generation if we intend to bond with the inheritance. Millennials join this generation with a promise to move us closer to Reformation. Whether they realize this role or not, it is their highest definer.

We have sacrificed principle, process, and protocol for the past five generations at the expense of legitimacy and authenticity. We have done so to prove that we are experts at losing the very youth we attempt to please. We have worked very hard at perfecting "prodigalism." The road behind us is strewn full, in both ditches, of the carcasses of destinies! We have perfected the art of emptying church of kingdom culture. Wasted inheritance abounds.

Our marvelously celebrated "answers to the wrong questions" have emptied the kingdom of Kingdom itself. We have put the King into exile so we could fix all that we considered inappropriate in His original design of Ecclesia and architecture of kingdom. We started this process by removing Ecclesia from the Kingdom. We simply announced one day that we are in the Church Age. From that moment on, we put ourselves in charge of defining "church."

However, kingdom remains Kingdom. Being born of the spirit still brings you into the kingdom. Entering the kingdom still makes you a kingdom citizen. Maturity in the kingdom still makes you an inheritor! Becoming a Kingdom citizen is still about serving the King. Ignoring kingdom so we can serve our own agendas does not change Kingdom. Kingdom does not go away. Kingdom is not an exercise in "being served by the King's sacrifice." Kingdom is becoming a living sacrifice who is abandoned to serving the King. God does not serve us. We serve God.

The Kingdom reset that we are in as I write this manifesto demands a return to the Biblical principles, processes, and protocols that form the Kingdom culture.

Looking for another way is treason. The work of those hoping to cash in on church and a further betrayal the purposes of the Father is Judas Iscariot all over again. I have no more time for discussions on how to make Judas comfortable in his treason. Modern Judas asks, "What is in this for me?" Modern Judas leaders ask, "What is in this for my career?"

Kingdom is about the purposes of the King. He is the Inheritor of the Inheritance. He intends to rule All. He has a strategy to do so through His representative inheritors.

The original design and definition of ekklesia begins with Kingdom.

Kingdom Leaders at the Gates

When Alexander the Great conquered the world, he wept - according to Plutarch - because there remained nothing he could conquer that would make him even more "the master of a world." With that in mind, Alexander set about to put the mark of Greek culture on every conquered land and people. To bring Greek cultural influence into these nation states, he called an "apostolos" into his court and authorized him to carry the culture of his kingdom to these distant places.

He gave the apostle an assignment.

The apostle would represent the king personally. His duties would include admiralty of an armada of ships, financial investments the king would make through his assignment to secure kingdom assets, leadership and coordination of "oversight experts" (elders) in various facets of culture. The apostle would also lead an army, as a general, that accompanied him for protection and power. The army would help secure the purpose of the apostolic expedition and enforce the decrees of the king.

Arriving at the shores of a conquered land, the apostle and apostolic company would travel to the gates of a city-state polis. In the gates, they would present the bona fides from the king and prove that they represented him. The apostle would arrive at the gates with money, experts in culture, and a marching army. He would inform the authorities at the gates of his assignment.

The apostle would then stand in the main gates of the city. This was a building. This building included the entry and exit point of the walled city but represented the authorities that governed the region.

From this building, he would call the "ekklesia" of citizens from that polis. The citizens of the ecclesia had authority to accept or reject what the apostle announced. They judged the messenger and his message. They had the authority to accept or reject the assignment. They had authority to implement the King's decisions. This body was also tasked with problem-solving the process of implementation for the region.

They would accept or reject the apostle and his apostolic company. They would work with him or against him and his elders.

The Meaning of *Ekklesia*

The word, *ekklesia*, does not mean "called out." This is commonly, nearly pervasively, assumed for legitimate reasons. While the prefix, *ek*, can mean "out," it can also mean "into" or "unto." In fact, it always infers "into" even when it means "out of." In this case, the compound means "called together into or unto assembly." Assembling means assembled with the connotation of pieces put together to form the whole.

The common evangelical meaning of "called out of the world" does not appear as a meaning for *ekklesia* anywhere in Scripture.

It is a legitimate idea. It is validated in the reality that we come out of the Kingdom of darkness and enter the Kingdom of light. When we speak of "coming out," we are speaking of coming in. We speak of "kingdom transfer." We are called into as much as we are called out of. The "called out" are actually "called into."

"You must be born from above to **enter the Kingdom of God**." (Jesus to Nicodemus, emphasis mine.)

The Greeks had another word to communicate the idea of "called out." It usually applied to party, celebration, feast, or occasion of important such as a wedding.

In fact, *"ekklesia"* is a technical term for a people "called together into assembly." It infers a judicial and legislative activity. *Ekklesia* involves making decisions and solving problems by judgment, voting, or an acquiescing process. Those assembled accept or reject ideas and strategies present to a group of representative leaders. They have the authority (keys) to allow or disallow.

(Neither children nor the simple minded would participate or be a part of the assembly. Non-citizens would also be excluded from participation. It was a serious moment with serious outcomes.)

G. W. Kirby, discussed the use of the word, *"ekklesia"* in the Greek translation of the Old Testament. His focus was its use in speaking of times when Israel "gathered before the Lord for religious purposes." Mr. Kirby points out that the Jews had been 'called out' from the nations to be God's special people. Yet, even here the scholar misses the greater point, that the people were called together more than were called out. Congregation is the whole culture. Ecclesia is "called to appear before the Lord" to represent Him in war, judgment, and cultural normalization.

The idea of being called out of the world has left many believers with the false impression that they were not called to assemble. This error empties many relationship to their a regional Ecclesia or even attendance to some aspect of a building, body or bride. They believe that they are the church all by themselves. Some believe their families can be a church, at home. Some believe that the *"ekklesia,"* as a term, has no relevant meaning in modern times at all. Some think a 'micro' church is a valid concept. Some say 'a two or three' is a church.

The Ecclesia is "called to," and the "calling to" is a matter of construction, expansion, and building as Jesus makes clear in Matthew 16.

So even when we consider the *ek* of *ekklesia* as "out," we end up with the wrong conclusion, especially if we make the wrong assumptions. We conclude that "out" is an adequate descriptor of the Building, Body, and Bride. It is not. What is called out must also be called into.

No one can be the Ecclesia. That is nonsensical. The *ekklesia* Jesus builds is not only separate but intentionally expansive. It demonstrably destructive of the positions held by God's enemies!

The Ecclesia is selected, elected, chosen, positioned, called, and appointed from within the Kingdom of God. It is believers who are part of the Kingdom by spiritual birth called into prepared positions for spiritual representation.

The Ecclesia is a Remnant within nations. A Remnant within the Remnant will soon expand in influence. They will rise with New Era Reformation in their hearts and a cry for Reform in their mouths. The Ecclesia in nations will respond with the greatest kingdom reset of history!

Jesus builds believers into His Ecclesia so they represent Him as the Kingdom of Heaven in the Earth. He is not establishing community. He is establishing culture.

Whatever may be inferred by the term "community" would be better defined by use of the term "culture." And, whatever might be said of community begins with the establishing of culture. One thing is certain, to begin with community results in the sacrifice of cultural foundations.

The kingdom keys do not establish commonality since it is already established in and by the culture. Whatever is common among the kingdom citizenry, in any sense of community, can be better identified in the principle, process, and protocol that is kingdom culture. This is what is allowed or not allowed by the Ecclesia.

The Ecclesia Jesus constructs carries Kingdom keys.

The Greek *Ekklesia* and the Hellenistic Era

The Kingdom Keys release into earth what has already been decreed in heaven. The sense of the verb is periphrastic. Jesus the King decides. The Ecclesia has authorization to set that into place in history as His people in a place.

Acts 2:42 says, "They devoted themselves to the apostle's *Didache*, shareholding, eating meals together, and involved intercession." The apostolic Didache, or apostolic preaching and teaching, is an announcement of the King's cultural norms.

When Jesus says, "Seek first the Kingdom of God **and His righteousness**," [emphasis mine] He refers directly to the culture of the Kingdom. The Ruler has rules.

The apostle would stand in the main gates and announce the decrees of the King. The ekklesia would hear the announcement. They would then accept or reject the announced intentions communicated to them through the apostle. He personally and specifically represented the king. Rejecting him meant rejecting the king.

Jesus is very clear about this: "Whoever listens to you, listens to Me. Whoever rejects you, rejects Me. Whoever rejects Me, rejects the One who sent Me." (Luke 10:16)

If the decrees announced by the apostle were rejected, the army could respond one of three ways.

- They could attack the main gates and simply carry out the king's desire to alter the present leadership.
- They could wipe the whole lot of them off the face of the earth.
- They could install leadership that would agree to carry out the king's wishes.

The apostle could only represent the king once he was sent by the conquering king and positioned in the gates. He would always arrive with all that was necessary to carry out the king's decrees. Positioning kingdom leaders at the gates comes through the King's apostolic representative. The leadership structure of the existing culture would shift because elders would begin oversight functions in the polis. (The regional center of government and culture.)

Alexander wished all the conquered lands to emulate Greek culture. The apostle arrived with elders. Elders were men and women of expertise and experience in various aspects of Greek culture. They would train the people of the city-state or polis in Greek culture. They would problem-solve the transition and transformation. They would have oversight of the establishing of the king's cultural expectations and anticipations. (This is what is meant by "law and prophets.)

Specifically, they would teach the existing culture how to do business, educate and train, operate in courts of law, settle disputes, build buildings with Greek architectural influence, teach everyone to speak and write *Koine* Greek (the "common" Greek of everyday life and general discourse), and, in short, follow the principles, processes, and protocols of Greek culture.

This expansion of Greek culture became known as "Hellenization."

Historic aspects of this cultural influence aside, Hellenization pushed Greek and Jewish culture and civilization into an intense dialogue about culture that resulted in the cultural condition of Jesus' day. (This prevailed in the occupation of Rome.)

This push produced the translation of the Old Testament from Hebrew into *Koine* Greek called "the Septuagint." This document remains our oldest copy of Law and Prophets, the translation quoted by Jesus, and the translation the New Testament quotes of the Old. The cultural "creep" continued, influencing Jewish culture and literature. ("Cultural creep" is the progressive influence one culture makes within another when one culture is strongly influenced by another.)

Cultural creep is the strategy of kingdom culture!

Use of the phrase "cultural creep" would be appropriately applied to understanding the syncretism of Roman Catholicism. It accommodates cultures instead of confronting them. Where it is allowed, worship, superstition, and erroneous worldviews enter church-anity. This is the very opposite intention of kingdom, its culture, and Ecclesia.

This syncretism resulted in prayers to saints as a means of praying to the ancestors. It normalized idolatry and made demons into patron saints. It blended calendars so that heathen moon and sun worship became part of the Roman Catholic schedules. All this violates God's Word and kingdom culture. (I offer this as an example of how church-anity did exactly opposite of what Jesus intends.)

In the days of Jesus, common Greek language and Hellenistic culture were enjoying a period of great expansion under Roman rule. The New Testament reveals adaptations to literary Greek traditions. (As opposed to Israel's errant culture.) The writing of plays, epic poems, lyric poems in the Greek language and style were becoming more commonly accepted among the Jews. This carried over into syntax and word choices Holy Spirit made for the Gospels and Epistles, and into word choices within John's Revelation. Even today, Israel yields to literary examples from Jewish authors who adopt Hellenistic literary forms.

Ecclesia in Operation

As soon as the *ekklesia* agreed to the king's decrees, the elders who accompanied Alexander's apostle would begin to work with the leaders in the city gates. The apostolic elders would gain full entrance to the entire region, inside and outside, from this entry and exit point of government. They would become kingdom leaders at the gates. That's is the gates of the city each had specific purposes that often matched the cultural and commercial operations of the polis.

The money the king sent with the apostle to begin to establish Greek cultural influence was distributed by the apostle. This speaks to the picture of people "laying money at the feet of the apostles." (Acts 4:35) The elders would apply funds to the points of influence, building, fine arts, music and dance, writing and publishing, acting and debating, judging and justice, doing business and expanding commerce.

The Army protected the Apostle and his company. The oversight elders became part of the new operating system forming in the city-state or polis through this kingdom influence. The apostle brought expertise and experience with him. The apostolic company presented Greek culture to the existing culture. They established it through influence.

An *ekklesia* always responded to the authorities in the gates. Leaders had authority to call together into assembly. They operated from a position of authority. These were the kingdom leaders at the gates. So, the apostle maintains leadership without a hand off. Elders apply and implement the mission. All function from the gates, displacing through cultural influence the existing commissioners of culture.

Apostle Jesus Builds His Ecclesia

When Jesus sends an apostle to a region, the apostle arrives with provision, elders, and an angelic army. He faces the prevailing spiritual conditions. Rulers, authorities and cosmic dominators who produce the present darkness and spiritual conditions of that region confront him. [See Ephesians 6.] The "present darkness" is the prevailing spiritual condition of the region.

He presents his *bona fides* at the main gates. He can be positioned in the gates because the One who sends the Apostle has superior, universal authority in Heaven and the Earth. He is positioned in those spiritual gates to announce the mind of the King who sent him. He is positioned to oversee the full implementation of an assignment.

The apostle manifests spiritual authority, power, and wisdom. He is the blueprint carrier of the King's strategy. His purpose is to influence the city-state toward its redemptive purpose. Its redemptive purpose is what it looks like when fully transformed. Purpose is revealed when it functions as one of the redeemed cultures of Messiah's inheritance.

Jesus says, "I will build My Ecclesia." He envisions the exact specifications of what that assembly looks like, and how it functions. He builds His Ecclesia by positioning kingdom leaders to represent Him in the region. He gives them the authority to accept or reject His mandate for the region. He authorizes them to prepare and position kingdom leaders at the gates. He knows that they will prepare and position people the King can call into assembly as a kingdom Ecclesia. He prepares and positions these people with the King's blueprints. He prepares and positions living building stones, operating body parts, and proper adorning for a bride.

The kingdom keys are given to these leaders and extended to the entire Ecclesia when it is matured in stature. Kingdom keys only operate at the regional Ecclesia level when a kingdom culture is in place. Keys displace the strategically positioned authorities of Hades that were previously occupying the main gates. Apostles overcome these authorities to begin the process. The Ecclesia finishes the displacement by its expansion of kingdom culture influence.

The gates of Hell carried influence into the main gates. From that position, they enabled their own ecclesia. By their authority and influence, they produced a dark culture. That culture carried a special characteristic. The character of the prevailing spiritual condition marks the culture of the region. The control or influence mechanism is manifested in the existing culture.

When the apostle arrives at the main gates, he would first overwhelm existing rulers. They will lose their authority to assemble their own ekklesia as kingdom culture influence expands. They will no longer maintain influence to determine what is allowed or disallowed. The apostle would then begin the process to reset the *polis* with kingdom culture. He does this with spiritual power and authority. The Ecclesia expands the kingdom culture in the existing culture.

Establishing a kingdom Ecclesia within a kingdom culture answers to "I will build My *ekklesia.*"

"Building My Ecclesia," as Jesus puts it, displaces the entrenchments of the present prevailing spiritual conditions. It places a new "called together into assembly" of kingdom cultural leaders in superior position of influence. These leaders determine what is or is not allowed. They disallow the cultural norms of darkness by spiritual influence.

When Christ commissioned His originating kingdom leaders - **the Great Commission** - we can be absolutely certain He had this in mind:

"I have all authority in Heaven and Earth [I have conquered the cosmic order known as "the world system," and I want My culture to dominate every culture].

"As you are going [wherever you are going on assignment], disciple cultures."

"Bury them in baptism in the Name and Authority of the ruling Father, Son, and Holy Spirit [for individual discipling and personal lifestyle change]."

"Train them to obey all I have commanded you [to announce in the city gates of the cultures to which I assign you]."

"Don't lose sight of this: I will continue My involvement with you until time reaches ultimate [perhaps, until you finish this job]."

Jesus dismantles the influence of Greek culture to restore the culture of the kingdom. He would influence with superior, authentic kingdom principles, processes, and protocols.

The culture of the Kingdom of God is not Hebrew. It is a fulfillment of what that culture was designed to produce. Fullness and fulfillment of that culture comes in a spiritually-matured and grace-gifted people, empowered by Holy Spirit. They prepared and positioned by kingdom leadership dynamics as a building, body, and bride.

Context

I have been discussing this viewpoint of *ekklesia* for a couple of decades. This discussion seems radical to people imaging modern forms of "church-anity." What they learn from the church growth paradigms and the ever-changing evangelical continuum looks nothing like what Jesus says. Church growth paradigms see church as the accumulation of believers. Most of the people with this viewpoint immediately turn down the volume on this discussion. If someone starts talking kingdom, they go into "la-la-la-la" mode. The avoidance behavior is bizarre.

We cannot know the authentic meaning of *ekklesia*, however, if we dismiss the Kingdom. The word, *ekklesia*, loses nearly all its meaning when it has no Kingdom context. When we remove ekklesia from kingdom, we can make church anything we design and define it to be. While that might make people happy, it asks the King not to rule or even enter His own king-

We cannot ignore the effort of moderns to make the Word line up with doctrinal systems. It has great power in improperly defining modern church-anity. We deal with this limitation to the meaning of the Bible as aberrant. We remove its limitation. We move past it to get to originality so we hear the voice of Jesus.

We listen to Jesus talk. We hear Him say, "I will build My *ekklesia*, and the gates of *hades* will not withstand My construction. I give you kingdom keys to allow and disallow on Earth what has already been allowed and disallowed in Heaven." (Mathew 16:18-19)

I am aware that I am ignoring the discussion of Simon as a pebble and Jesus as the Gibraltar.

"You are Peter. On this rock, I will build." Simon says to Jesus, "You are the Son of the God who lives." Jesus uses his name as a point of reference to foundations. That is authentic, of course, but does nothing to define the word "*ekklesia*" in Jesus' mouth.

I think that we can agree, that if we listen to the words of Jesus, it will be difficult for us to separate *ekklesia* from Kingdom. Kingdom keys and the Ecclesia He builds are inseparable in His mind.

There are some great minds that assumed that the word just "came to mean" a get-together for believers. In the same way, some now think any one or two believers in the same place at the same time is an *ekklesia*. "Goodie for Jesus Tupperware" parties are not displacing hell's entrenched territorial demons or driving out this present darkness. Café latte for three isn't shutting down abortion clinics. "Every let's take some time to share now" gathering is not *ekklesia*. All of that is cool. It is kingdom culture in action. It is not the church.

The truth is that Jesus builds a Kingdom assembly from within His Kingdom. The Ecclesia He builds uses matured saints prepared and positioned to function, submitted to individual assignment, never wavering or distracted by other ideas. This assembly releases into the Earth what Heaven decides about entire regions! It is empower kingdom leaders to displace the strategically positioned authorities of Hades. It is Kingdom come, Kingdom culture, Kingdom conquest. It ain't your mamma's church.

Ekklesia did not mean "called-out." There was, in fact, another word for that kind of public gathering. The prefix "*ek*" also means "into." Ekklesia was used to speak of the representatives of a polis, or the body of people, who assembled to make judicial, legislative and cultural decisions as a governmental authority.

The meaning of the word never related to our modern concept of "church." It is a kingdom word. It helps our understanding that this word, polis, was also used in the translation of the Old Testament. Jesus was clearly well versed in this Greek translation. It says that God's people were called together into assembly before the Lord. That meaning is consistent with the words of Jesus in His meaning for *ekklesia* and *apostolos*.

The relevant revelation of *ekklesia* is that it functions as the Kingdom on Earth, that it represents the Kingdom in Heaven in its Earthly form. It reflects the manifestation of a spiritual reality in a physical world. God has a Heavenly Kingdom. He wants an Earthly kingdom. God has a Heavenly Ecclesia. God wants an Earthly Ecclesia.

Regional Ecclesia

So, why would I say, "regional Ecclesia?" Why would I entitle the entire discussion "regional Ecclesia?"

A great deal of discussion has been given to city-church. In fact, some definitive statements have been made about what the Bible recognizes as an "Ecclesia." Some leaders make assumptions about "one city, one church." The basis for these statements isn't definitive. Some make statements in an outside the Bible context.

We are creating a Bible and historical context

right now. We are fitting Ecclesia within it. The assumptions of "one city, one church" do not fit the context. I have heard friends say, "The Bible never speaks of the church as anything other than one church in one city." We must, however, return to the premise. What does that word "church" mean in the mouth of the person speaking it or writing it? We must also ask what the word "*polis*" means? Bible records refer to Ecclesia by place and name. There is an assumption that modern city names dictate how we think about the definition of an Ecclesia because of a mis-perception about the names of regional city-states.

The word "*polis*" does not refer to the same thing to which we refer when we say, "city." *Polis* refers to people associated together culturally based on a commonality of association with geographic locality. The location and people are not defined by city walls. The word *polis* isn't a metropolitan or village word. It is a governmental and political word. It describes how people in a region govern themselves by a mutually-beneficial union. They sacrifice some independence to gain some security. They benefit corporately by sacrificing personally. This is important because Kingdom has a culture. The focus of the Great Commission is kingdom leadership that disciples cultures.

The most consistent point of reference by

which to grasp the Biblical concept of an Ecclesia is "God's purpose for a people in a place." Begin here to understand the meaning of Ecclesia as a regional expression of kingdom authority.

Consider that Ecclesia in Israel referred to a people who were together in a place. They were a congregation if we consider only how many were hanging out. They were an Ecclesia when the men of the inheritance tribes were called before the Lord. God replaces them in a defined land. His people of a place secure His purpose for that place. Israel is a representative culture at this point in history. What God wanted for every culture, He put into one culture.

Knowing God's purpose for a place and people is the very essence of apostolic blueprinting. God influences a place with a people. His positions a Remnant to influence existing culture with kingdom culture. In this way, that place can produce its purpose.

The Kingdom of Heaven is a people influencing places on Earth as the people of Heaven. The citizens of that Kingdom are called together into assembly to agree with the judgment decisions of the King they represent. The spiritual influence of that Kingdom increases through their oneness. The spiritual influence of His Kingdom displaces existing spiritual conditions. The Ecclesia judges what God wants and establishes it spiritually within the kingdom. Overcoming spiritual power and authority releases that through the Kingdom. The culture of that Kingdom impacts the existing culture by spiritual influence.

Apostle and Ecclesia

In the book, Apostle, I explain how the technical term, ekklesia, speaks to cultural influence and impact. Further, I define how the Kingdom meaning of these ideas fits the mission of the apostles with apostolic teams. I define how apostles originate but the entire Ecclesia requires eldership, or oversight, from kingdom leadership dynamics.

For our purposes here, let me say that Jesus as King wants His Kingdom culture to influence and impact Earth's cultures. He sees those cultures redeemed. He has a strategy to do so through spiritual Kingdom come, Kingdom culture, and Kingdom conquest.

Ecclesia is best understood as regional. This manifesto assumes that Kingdom operates with these cultural principles, processes, and protocols in mind. We will discuss "regional" in greater detail later on in ***Regional Ecclesia Manifesto***.

Printed in Great Britain
by Amazon